OWN YOUR AMAZON

CHANNEL OP'S JOURNEY
TO MANAGING BRANDS ON THE WORLD'S
— LARGEST MARKETPLACE —

TYLER METCALF

BRIGHTRAY
PUBLISHING®

We help busy professionals write and publish their stories
to distinguish themselves and their brands.

(407) 287-5700 | Winter Park, FL
info@BrightRay.com | www.BrightRay.com

ISBN: 978-1-7357861-6-2

Published in the United States of America.
BrightRay Publishing ® 2023

TABLE OF CONTENTS

For Elaine

and our crew!

INTRODUCTION

When I was in the third grade, my dad and uncle Scott started a lawn care business, aerating lawns around Ogden, Utah, my hometown. Utah is most known for being quiet, Mormonism, and our 1990s Jazz basketball team—as you can imagine, there just wasn't much to do growing up. The most fun I ever had as a kid was running around in an open field with my friends, building forts out of any materials we found lying around. Hoping to give me something more productive to do, my dad quickly roped me, his oldest son, into helping him with his lawn business throughout the spring as the flag boy, a job where I placed tiny flags in clients' lawns next to sprinkler heads. I made a buck per house, so if we did ten houses in a day, I made ten bucks, which, hey, is pretty good money for a third-grader.

Even though I liked simply helping my dad out, I quickly discovered where the real money was in the operation, and I knew I couldn't make it by playing flag boy. My dad and I made a deal. If I went door-to-door pitching our aeration services, I'd make ten dollars for every house I sold. Needless to say, I got pretty good at sales at a young age. By the end of the spring season, I'd always have plenty of cash to spend during the summer.

I had one of my best sales days during a fundraising event for my grandmother's church. I went out with a bunch of the other boys from the church, and each one of them was too terrified to knock on strangers' doors. Since I had loads of practice and was more than comfortable with this, I ran circles around the neighborhood that afternoon, knocking on doors with a trail of boys behind me everywhere I went. By the end of the day, I had sold about thirty houses. My dad, of course, complained about how I happened to sell so well on a day we couldn't even make a dime.

Eventually, when I got older, my dad and uncle had me working the aeration machine, and I began making about $50 each afternoon and more than $200 a weekend. Having the extra cash was always a plus, especially when my friends and I would play cards, but one of the most fulfilling perks of my dad and uncle's business was working together with people I admired. We had a solid business model, and I felt like my work held value. And as much as it was work, it was also a lot of fun. I made some of my best memories by planting those flags and selling our services.

Despite how much dedication I put into the lawn aerating business, I didn't have the same patience for my school work as most of it felt like a total and complete waste of time. Now, this isn't me bragging: I was actually a super bright kid back in the day. In kindergarten, I only missed one question on the 300-question exam to get into Ogden's magnet program, a test the majority of kids couldn't pass. I really was smart! I say all of this just to state: despite my enormous potential, I still never did my homework to the despair of my parents and all of my teachers. Maybe I shouldn't admit this, but I had a really great high school friend, Mike, who always did his assignments. He would hand me his papers at the beginning of class so I could copy everything down. My teachers, who knew I never did my homework and instead copied Mike, always felt a strange mixture of surprise and frustration when grading my tests. Even if I didn't complete their assignments, I always aced the material when it actually mattered to me. My problem wasn't retaining the class information; I just hated doing the pointless busy work.

Even as an adult, I'm always looking for ways to save myself time and cut out inefficiencies. When earning my undergraduate degree, I worked as a temp at Goldman Sachs for a year. I operated in a small room, scanning documents with a few coworkers. Sometimes, these documents would be over a hundred pages and incredibly thick, and they had to be separately scanned for each entry into a DOS system. If you needed seven separate scans of the document in the system, you would have to scan that hundred-page document seven times—that is, if you only did as you were taught.

I could work unlimited overtime during the summer, so when I wasn't taking classes, I'd work sixty-hour weeks and even go in on the weekends. The weekends were when I did my experimenting, blasting music as I worked alone in the empty building. Before long, I figured out how to scan a document multiple times with one scan, along with a range of other tricks. I scanned four times quicker than anyone had ever done in the department, and everyone began to take notice.

My bosses finally asked me how I could scan everything at such a fast pace, and I encountered a dilemma: do I tell them all of my secrets, or do I keep them to myself? One of my tips was so helpful that I immediately coughed it up, figuring it could save my coworkers a lot of headaches. Although I did keep a few tricks close to my chest, I ended up telling them to everyone when I left the job. In the end, it felt better to share those with the team instead of leaving them to figure everything out for themselves.

As I said before, I had a knack for sales and improving all kinds of procedures (something adults used to call "cutting corners" but now, in the professional world, call "process optimization" and "a solution-oriented mindset"), but I really learned to apply these skills while working with a company called River Runners. With a specialization in toy sales, River Runners used Amazon as their online marketplace. Shocking, I know, but these were the early days of Amazon when many businesses weren't aware they should be expanding their online presence. Businesses focused more on brick-and-mortar stores than Amazon to the point that if you "did Amazon," you didn't tell people you "did Amazon."

As part of my job, I'd attend the Toy Fair in New York to comb the floor for prospective clients. Time and time again, I'd bring up Amazon only to hear companies proudly stick to their brick-and-mortar roots, saying, "Yeah, we don't really do that." Yet, many of these toy companies had online retailers that would place product orders and ship them directly to their warehouses, which would then sell on Amazon as a backdoor way of selling online. The toy companies had no idea how much money was being made off of their products. Talking to sales representatives on the phone, they'd be surprised that so many people in Logan, Utah wanted to buy kites. In reality, that's where one of the biggest retailers on Amazon stored their inventory in warehouses. Most of the time, you never told anyone you sold on Amazon. You simply bought a company's product and then sold it on the site, leaving the brands completely unaware of all the money from Amazon sales.

Upon learning and engaging with this, I quickly realized that I did not want to continue participating in the wholesale-retail model. This was not the way I wanted to do business, reselling products on Amazon. I wanted to be much more upfront with these brands and build partnerships with them.

Around 2016, I started my company, Channel Op, as an avenue to those goals. Before Amazon became synonymous with online shopping, I didn't feel concerned about market competition as I paraded around trade show floors as my company's only salesman, telling people about the opportunities a solid Amazon page could lead to. I, along with some of my brand managers, would walk the floors, shake hands, and explain our services. We'd enable brands to build their presence on Amazon, and we'd provide them with the tools to remain at the top of Amazon's search results. Even now, we cater all of our services to make sure that, no matter what your product is, it has the best representation on Amazon.

I write this book now as a guide for anyone who is interested in selling or currently sells on Amazon, as well as any budding entrepreneurs struggling with team management or process development. Hopefully, someone somewhere can learn about my experiences, tricks of the trade, and yes, even stupid decisions and walk away with a better idea of what they want their company to stand for. In the following pages, I'm ready to lay out how Channel Op always does its best to meet employee and client needs, how you can build your own brand's identity on Amazon, and how, at the end of the day, everything comes down to relationships, relationships, relationships.

Unlike when I spent every day in a cramped high school desk or working at Goldman Sachs, I promise I won't hold anything back.

CHAPTER 1

THE START
OF CHANNEL OP

When you navigate to a little website called Amazon.com, you almost always expect to find a perfectly manicured product page that is full of relevant information laid out in succinct bullets. The photographs of the product are abundant and capture it from all sides. The page is clear, organized, and accurate, no matter if you're looking for a phone charger or a barbecue grill.

Believe it or not, this wasn't always the case.

When I started Channel Op, you'd be lucky to find a product's page without a low-resolution .jpeg or a single-sentence description. Not many sellers understood that Amazon was only going to get bigger, so when I approached prospects, I always made sure they realized that their business' presence on the website was an extension of their brands. In some cases, it is a brand's main presence. By the start of 2016, I had my first five clients, and by the end of the year, I had 34 clients.

My pitch to these companies was not completely tied up in raising sales on Amazon. I also helped them protect those brick-and-mortar relationships they had built over the years. Around this same time, people began to realize their products were being resold on Amazon for lower prices. These third-party sellers were undercutting prices by even a few cents to become the primary sellers. While brands were fighting a battle on Amazon, brick-and-mortar shops began losing sales altogether. People would walk into a Circuit City or Radioshack, look at a product they wanted to buy, and then check the price on Amazon. More often than not, it was cheaper on Amazon, and physical retailers would lose out.

This, in part, is why even bigger brands began to take Amazon more seriously. Being based in Park City, Utah like Channel Op, I saw Skullcandy's relationship with Best Buy tested by their Amazon presence. Best Buy threatened to minimize its shelf space unless Skullcandy started to police its pricing on Amazon. For a huge brand like Skullcandy, this was manageable, but what about the rest of the sellers on Amazon?

When it comes down to what services Channel Op offers, it is ultimately peace of mind. We'll run advertising and grow your brand's presence on Amazon. We will fix up all of your product pages and make sure the pages look the way your brand wants them to look. We help to police your channel, making sure it's cleaner and the competition is fair. A huge, yet often overlooked, part of our job is also strategically stocking product inventory, which ensures you sell more. In the early days, one of these trigger points would clearly resonate with the brands we sought out. If not, it was most likely because the brand wasn't on Amazon yet and would need our help to launch its page. I realized early on that to give all of the different brands the attention they needed, I needed a much bigger team.

The Beginnings of the Channel Op Team

For a pretty long time, I acted as my company's only salesman, walking the show floors and managing the brands. I quickly realized I needed some help with the grind of Amazon. By a stroke of luck, I knew a friend of a friend who was starting up an eCommerce outsourcing company in the Philippines. Since I needed some assistants to help me with managing brands, rather than full-on brand managers who could do the whole process themselves, I decided to give my friend's company a try. I ended up hiring some amazing people. Even from the beginning, our Philippines team has always been the backbone of Channel Op. As the ultimate problem-solving, kick-butt squad, our team in the Philippines grew to nine in just the first year.

In a few short months, I needed more than assistants to help with tasks. I needed people who could act as points of contact for clients. For this to work, though, I'd have to train them face to face, not over the Internet like with my Philippines team. So, I started hiring in Park City. The training process typically looked like me buying a laptop for a new employee and then having them sit next to me for a week. As I went through my day managing clients, I'd talk the employee through everything I did. Then, when I felt they were ready, I let them manage one or two clients to start off. They always knew that I encouraged them to ask me questions along the way. Okay, maybe my training program wasn't exactly foolproof, but it did seem to work.

We were a ragtag team, but our numbers slowly grew. Being a part of the first few people hired by a startup, there is a "we are in this together, fighting in the trenches" mentality. It all comes together in a beautiful sort of way, especially when employees start to find their grooves. Two of my early employees, Britney and Wiley, were the first to really understand Channel Op's mission. With only a few months on the job, they were able to manage clients without much supervision. They were hustlers, and they made those early days possible, giving clients the attention they deserved. It takes way more than a capable crew to handle the day-to-day of Amazon, though. As a website and online marketplace, Amazon has its own idiosyncrasies that can be (for the lack of a better term) exploited to bring more attention to your brand. I learned about some of these tools during my time with River Runners and was able to apply them for years before Amazon fixed the issues.

A Willingness to Experiment

Amazon's advertising was truly in its infancy at the beginning of Channel Op. They eventually rolled out features that were only available to Vendor Central, not Seller Central. Vendor Central is for suppliers directly selling to Amazon in bulk, while Seller Central is for merchants who directly sell to their customers. Vendors were given better ad placement options with banner ads, which were not available to sellers. Always looking for better ways to position our clients' advertisements, I found I was able to create a Vendor Seller account with a burner email address to gain access to these ads. Soon, our cost per click was much lower and our conversion rate was much better, outperforming the market in comparison to other sellers.

Another "tool" we took advantage of involved shipping logistics for restocking warehouses. Amazon will try to route shipments to multiple destinations in order to streamline its shipping process, making sure that products go to different warehouses to serve varying population centers. So, if you wanted to ship 240 units to Memphis, Tennessee, Amazon would send half of the units to California and the other half to warehouses in Pennsylvania with a minority of units going to the closest warehouse. I figured out fairly early on that, if you told the system you only wanted to send one unit, it would only send to one destination. Once that destination was set, you could modify the number of units you were sending to 240. Now, instead of moving boxes from warehouse to warehouse ourselves, Amazon would pay for the shipping. I don't blame Amazon for eventually closing this loophole, but it did save my clients hundreds of dollars on every shipment.

Not every tool we had in those early days of Channel Op was at the expense of Amazon. Our clients experienced the benefits of video ads as soon as Amazon introduced them, solely because competitors were slow to pick up on their importance. On average, a good Rest of World (ROW) advertisement will net you $3 to $5 for every dollar you spend. Our early video ad campaigns averaged about $15 to $20 in sales per ad. For the first 18 months of their introduction, our brands took advantage of video ads while other brands sat on their hands. All it took was a solid 30-second video of the product, which was sometimes just pulled from the brand's explainer video for the product. With that, we were getting prime placement for a low cost per click on Amazon search results.

The key to handling Amazon's ecosystem is the willingness to experiment, which has been built into Channel Op's DNA from the beginning. There were less clever ways to make sales, though. A problem then, and a problem now, lies in "brands" buying thousands of reviews every month in order to keep up with competitors. It was a common practice prior to October 2016 and I tried to discourage it, but even I admit to playing the game. Even though we had to be on par with other agencies and provide the service, I never believed in it as a solution. When you think about it, a company throwing money at the problem isn't very effective or fulfilling. There's no "job well done" feeling, and let's be real: it just feels scummy. To this day, there are legacy reviews that have never been cleared, so reviews bought six years ago are still around to this day. Some products with more than 30,000 reviews have a not-so-hidden advantage built in. If you haven't caught on yet, I felt extremely happy to stop offering the service once Amazon began cracking down on buying reviews.

Channel Op would rather organically build your brand, using tools in sometimes nontraditional ways to boost your presence on Amazon. Recalling those early days as a company, I feel prideful of where Channel Op is today and the level of service we provide our clients. No matter the product, we know that we'll get an Amazon page up and running that will do more than simply increase sales; it will make your whole brand strategy more effective.

CHAPTER 2

BASIC STEPS TO RUNNING AN AMAZON PRODUCT PAGE

If anyone tells you they have a silver bullet for success on Amazon... believe me, there isn't one. If you want to keep a product at the top of Amazon's ranking system, the secret sauce is repetition more than anything else. So, what does that repetition look like? For Channel Op, it means creating consistency in a week-to-week period so data can be analyzed and incorporated into inventory management and advertising.

When we take on a new client, we start by getting the lay of the land. This means obtaining all of the product data we can from the client, including SKU (Stock Keeping Unit) numbers, UPCs (Universal Product Codes), ASINs (Amazon Standard Identification Numbers), pricings, titles, bullet points, and product images. We scan through the spreadsheets and folders of photos they send us, and we take stock. Sometimes, brands come to us and have insufficient, or even incorrect, data. We make sure that everything is where it needs to be and check for any mistakes—especially with price listings. They have a small margin for error in spreadsheets. All it takes is one price in the wrong column to start throwing the numbers off, so we always double-check before we load the data into Amazon.

Once brand managers have the Amazon page basics locked in, the different teams begin their assignments. The creative team gathers all of the content necessary for the product page on the Amazon Marketplace. By optimizing the product page, they make it easier for customers to find and purchase the brand's products. This includes organizing the proper images, page titles, detailed bullets, and search terms. Our team in the

Philippines will design the storefront or any other A-plus content if the client doesn't already have it. This is all necessary to keep products higher up in the ranking system.

The Elusive Amazon Ranking System

Amazon's ranking system is known only to Amazon, so no one knows 100% for sure what dictates rank. That being said, there are a few factors that seem to stand out among the rest, the number one being sales. However, it's not solely measured by units sold; it's by total revenue. So, Amazon will weigh ten $10 unit sales the same as one $100 unit sale. Besides sales, the delivery speed will definitely nab you some favoritism. If the product is Prime, the one-day delivery will go a long way compared to that same product with merchant-fulfilled delivery. In a tight third place comes reviews. Reviews have to be above four stars; otherwise, your ranking will drop. You might even find your ads aren't placed as much. Again, no one knows Amazon's lines of demarcation for sure, but these are the top three factors necessary just to be competitive in the marketplace.

While the creative team focuses on the product page and its conversion, the advertising team ensures the product gets in front of the right customers. Channel Op will set up, optimize, and manage the various Amazon advertising channels. We make sure products are easily found, all while minimizing costs. Once we start tracking data, the advertising team can see what keywords have the highest conversion rates.

A brand's name should offer up a first-mover advantage in its advertising. When placing ads, Amazon takes into account your conversion rate on those keywords, so you can possibly bid less. Again, there is currently no way to verify this, but it does feel like if you convert really well on a keyword, you can bid less and still win out versus competitors. Say I am a sunscreen brand, and I really want to go up against Coppertone. I could overbid on the word "Coppertone" and still not score great placement, solely because Coppertone is converting so well on their own brand name. The big brands still have the advantage of gigantic ad budgets, but you can usually win on your own brand name if you're playing the game. It does become a "chicken or egg" situation because, in order to be at the top, you need to sell a lot, and in order to sell a lot, you need to be at the top. Having a solid budget does help because you can pay to be at the top of a lot of search results you wouldn't organically ever rank. Then, once you start converting, you won't have to pay as much as a percent of the overall sales.

Okay, so maybe Amazon will never outright say this, but your advertising does affect your organic ranking. If you buy ads and they convert—that's revenue. That revenue then impacts your organic ranking. It also seems the conversion rate on ad keywords does affect your conversion rate on an organic level as well. So, though Amazon may say there's a church-and-state divide between advertising and organic results, they're still intermingled. This is why we've seen Amazon put so much more investment into various ad types and ad placements in recent years. Though, once that organic conversion rate is high enough and there is a certain level of stability, brand managers and brands can start experimenting with finding new keywords.

Inventory Management: The Unsung Hero

With advertising and page optimization chugging along, Channel Op brand managers work hand in hand with brands to maintain that repetition. Consistency and attention to detail are necessary to keep your brand's sales optimized, and it all starts with inventory management—the least glamorous, yet most important, part of the job. The key is getting in stock and staying in stock. On top of that, there is both a science and an art to not overstocking or understocking. Every week, inventory should be reviewed, which doesn't necessarily mean shipping inventory. It's important to know where you stand. The goal for anyone managing inventory for Amazon is to have anywhere between six to eight weeks of inventory sitting in the channel at any given time.

No one wants to hear how important inventory management is on a sales pitch from us. It's not attractive or shiny—it is the block and tackle of getting the job done, meaning you need it for everything else to work. Staying in stock is key because if you're not, the product page will go dead. Advertisements will not run if you are not in stock, so there will be fewer eyes on your product. Without conversions on keywords and actual sales, your ranking will go down. It won't matter how on top of your advertisement campaigns you are or how well-designed your product page is. If you can't keep your product in stock, those efforts are wasted and the work won't matter.

With Channel Op, I have personally increased some brands' sales by 50% in six weeks simply by maintaining the stock, and the revenue increase alone was worth the price of admission for them.

When the machine is working and all the cogs mesh together, we are able to gather the metrics and data necessary for inventory forecasting. We send that data to the brands in the form of weekly progress reports, detailing what we're working on, the latest projects' updates, and recent figures. Eventually, the brands will receive a monthly "top down, bottom-up" report that includes more thorough data on how numbers are improving on a monthly and yearly basis. Channel Op takes inventory management forecasting pretty seriously. With six to 12 months of sales history and data, the team can start projecting inventory demands for the next year. Again, it's not flashy or fun, but you always need to be prepared.

We had one client have their product go viral in a video. Their entire inventory sold out over the next week. All of the inventory I had set aside for summer and a little bit into fall just disappeared. The brand continued to take some backorders on its own website, but they weren't back in stock for about eight months after the video dropped. Overall, the amazing week was not worth the eight months of inactivity. It's often those events you can't plan for that will take you by surprise, but you'll hopefully be ready for them.

Error Management

After everything is in stock, ads are running, and product pages are optimized, error management is the last step. At Channel Op, we monitor accounts daily to make sure content is current and listings are active. As I said before, we double-check that pricing is accurate and any fees involved are correct. If a problem rears its head, the team quickly responds to resolve the issue. Damaged or lost inventory is investigated, and claims are opened to make sure the client's sales aren't affected. Sometimes, Amazon changes its code in small ways. Say product pages aren't properly loading. Our teams know to jump on the phone with Amazon and have the patience to sit through some long calls before the issue is resolved.

The systems can be complicated, though, and some products don't lend themselves to easy-breezy inventory management. Clothing and shoes have various colors and sizes, so these are generally high SKU-count product lines. A single product, such as a sandal, may have 10 colors and sizes, making 100 SKUs right there that need to be checked every day. Each one of those sizes and colors will be bought at different rates as well. Medium and large sizes tend to go faster than small and extra large, which we have to factor into inventory management. You have to go over plenty of spreadsheets with a fine-toothed comb, but that's what it takes.

Every client of ours receives our undivided attention, but they are handled differently out of necessity. Generally, at Channel Op, we don't like to work with frozen food brands or furniture and large-scale appliance brands. Warehouse management and shipping become logistical nightmares, but if that's what you're into, all the power to you. Instead, we've had some of our greatest successes with beauty and personal care brands. The smaller packages for creams and lotions have long shelf lives and can be stored pretty easily in a warehouse. We've also had a good amount of success taking care of sports and outdoor brands, which may be because we're based out of Utah. At the end of the day, though, the basis for all of these brands' Amazon presences revolves around keeping them in stock.

Some of our favorite stories from Channel Op are about single solo entrepreneurs who are able to grow a brand from nothing to something. For them, going from $0 in revenue on Amazon to $5,000 a month in sales makes the largest possible difference in their lives. Some clients have been able to quit their part-time jobs and actually dedicate their time to their brands. If I've learned anything over the past decade, it's this: running an optimized Amazon brand strategy is attainable. You just need repetition and consistency to keep moving forward.

CHAPTER 3

THE BRANDS
WE SUPPORT

In this day and age, treating your clients with anything less than you'd hope to be treated with is the bare minimum. With all the brands we serve, I don't feel good delivering low-quality service, and I know my employees don't, either. That's why Channel Op's services go beyond just transactional management of a brand's Amazon account. We give every client a sense of ownership over their product page and Amazon presence. I know from experience that clients are much happier with the results when they can actually involve themselves in the process.

In the early days of Channel Op, I probably said yes to every brand that approached me for Amazon optimization. Now there are more factors, such as my team and its capacity, but it all comes down to wanting to work with people who treat each other with respect. It's only happened twice where someone on their kickoff call rudely spoke to the brand managers. As a general rule, Channel Op only works with brands that are eager to collaborate and maintain a professional attitude—a mindset, I'm happy to say, all of our current brands share.

Onboarding new brands with Channel Op is an exceptionally important phase within our process. We emphasize overcommunication to make sure brands and our brand managers are on the same page. It's different for every client, so flexibility is key to finding balance. We'll schedule those weekly phone calls for the first three weeks and then adjust as the client feels is necessary. Some like to be more hands-on, while others like to let us do our thing. We also use this step of the process to gather data, filling in any gaps for product listings on Amazon.

Solving early issues is sometimes what it takes to turn around a brand's page within the first month. We employ a range of software tools for monitoring and maintaining a brand's Amazon account while also ensuring various account settings are properly set up. We prioritize the key products or issues we need to attack first. If a brand has 1000 SKUs, we aren't going to fix all 1000 SKUs overnight. Through that initial triage, though, we may find a brand's bestsellers only have a single photo, and we can immediately make them look better with a new set of images. During the onboarding process, my team and I definitely take time to consider if we can majorly improve the brand's page in a short period. However, the key determining factor in whether or not we take on a brand is the rapport we build with it.

When I worked with past companies, our model was built on a wholesale-retail relationship; it was purely monetary. This never sat well with me because the people trying to sell their products didn't even benefit from the sale. We bought a brand's product and then sold it on Amazon. This separation from the brand usually resulted in errors in overstocking and understocking. Then, when we overstocked, we would end up discounting the product, which caused prices to decrease on Amazon. It was just bad business.

Starting Channel Op, I knew I wanted to redefine what that relationship with a brand could look like. This meant I had to sacrifice slightly on margin, but it would improve efficiency in general. We could directly work with a brand and not worry about having to force their price down like in the wholesale-retail model. By maintaining the inventory, we can retain a consistent price. Also, the brands are incentivized to help police anyone who's breaking those rules and discounting below the minimum advertised price (MAP). At the end of the day, everyone should receive slightly more margin because we're selling at MSRP 99% of the time (the other 1% being during promotions).

Building up the trust necessary for this kind of relationship starts as soon as we are introduced to a brand. Referrals and trade shows are our biggest avenues for meeting new clients, but we also work with brands that I've met through past business ventures and connections. The beauty of Channel Op's model is that I've gotten to know at least 300 business owners and executives over the past seven years, each with their own unique products and strategies.

Going Viral with FCTRY

Out of every brand Channel Op manages, I have the most history with FCTRY, a novelty toy company based in Brooklyn, New York. I first started managing FCTRY's brand back in my River Runner days and launched the company's premiere product, mustache pacifiers, on Amazon. We worked with them to list several successful and equally unique products, but I take the most pride in their "unicorn snot," a product that ranked as the number one body glitter on Amazon and still maintains that title to this day. Now, as a Channel Op client, FCTRY has many notable Amazon offerings. In fact, FCTRY owns some of my favorite product pages we've optimized to date, one of the most successful listings being their line of baby sunglasses. Up 30% in revenue year after year, FCTRY's success partially stems from its eagerness for experimentation. The company's CEO, Jason Feinberg, truly favors action over inaction, and oftentimes, we'll receive the go-ahead to try something new just to keep the ball rolling.

FCTRY is one of our brands that faces a unique challenge and opportunity rolled into one: inventory needs are almost impossible to predict. As a company, FCTRY wears its political beliefs on its sleeve. You can most prominently see this in their product line of political action figures, some of the most viral merchandise Channel Op has ever had the pleasure of working with. FCTRY's Ruth Bader Ginsberg action figure raised around $600,000 in production funds on Kickstarter, while its Bernie Sanders figure raised around $250,000—and the figures only became more popular in light of RBG's passing and Bernie's inauguration meme. Events like these increase the popularity of the action figures, which means maintaining stock keeps Channel Op's brand managers on their toes.

During the 2016 U.S. presidential election, FCTRY offered Hillary Clinton and Donald Trump action figures. We stocked about 10,000 figures in total, expecting to sell many during the election cycle. In one hour, we sold out the stock we thought would last us for a week. Overall, we ended up selling 50,000 units, five times more than we initially anticipated. Keeping up with FCTRY's inventory can be stressful when it's unpredictable, but at the same time, working with FCTRY and its products is fun. Jason's is one of the few brands we work with that consistently presents a new product line every year, and in general, his hit rate is reliable. Even when a product does miss, FCTRY's ability to pivot and move forward is unparalleled. Honestly, those first mustache pacifiers were a bigger hit than I initially thought they would be. Now, I think of Jason as a branding genius. FCTRY's products' packaging, prices, and names—it all makes sense and allows for FCTRY to dominate Amazon search results.

PARA'KITO: Du Français À L'américain

One of Channel Op's most long-standing relationships is with a mosquito repellent brand called PARA'KITO. I first met the company's general manager, Bastien Gauthier, in 2016 at Expo West. Bastien was the first person I ever approached who seemed ready to sign the contract on the floor. When I introduced myself and Channel Op's purpose, he responded, "When can we start?" Channel Op began managing his brand the very next week, and since then, we have nearly doubled PARA'KITO's sales every year.

PARA'KITO, being a mosquito repellent company with French headquarters, faces some unique challenges when facing Amazon's terms and conditions. As you can imagine, mosquito repellent sells better in the summer than in the winter. During the Zika virus outbreak in the summer of 2016, many people began stocking up on mosquito-repellent products, fearing they'd catch the virus. PARA'KITO saw a major uptick in sales, and after having a slow January, the company appreciated the boost in sales, as well as the fact that their products were being used for their intended purpose: to help protect customers from mosquito-borne diseases in an innovative, natural way.

With this increase in revenue from mosquito repellents, though, came an Amazon policy change. Amazon has always been careful about medical claims on product pages and, fearing some products would make false claims and not be completely legitimate, the platform began prohibiting the use of the words "Zika virus" in any titles, bullets, ads, keywords, or other copy. Amazon uses a "guilty until proven innocent" type of system. In the case of the Zika virus dilemma—and in many other cases we've encountered—Amazon will shut down your page first, then ask you to fix the errors. Luckily, Channel Op was able to identify the error, delete every instance of the words "Zika virus," and notify Amazon to republish the product page all in one afternoon.

PARA'KITO: Bastien Gauthier, General Manager[1]

Sometimes you make business decisions because you have facts, and other times, you make business decisions because you trust your gut. I'm happy PARA'KITO chose to trust Channel Op to support our brand on Amazon. When Tyler first approached me in 2016, there was no way to know how eCommerce would grow in the future, but he seemed so confident when talking about Amazon's strategy and how the platform could help us grow. PARA'KITO had always been a manufacturer; retailing, especially online, was not something we liked to do or knew how to do on our own. Tyler opened the door to us. He created our Amazon brand presence in the U.S., and after a while, he even began managing our European accounts. Since then, PARA'KITO has only grown alongside Channel Op.

PARA'KITO develops DEET-free, natural mosquito repellent products, our signature products being wearables like wristbands, sandals, and clips. Pesticide products have a lot of regulations tied to them and, being a French company with a presence in the U.S., we face many legal constraints. Amazon may be a global company, but it operates completely differently from one country to another. When Amazon began complying with EPA, which is like the FDA but for pesticide products, PARA'KITO already had all of the necessary documentation to prove its compliance as European regulations are much heavier than American regulations. Still, sharing those documents with Amazon was not simple; ping-ponging back and forth with Amazon took a lot of work, but Channel Op actually managed to do it successfully.

Every year, there are always new ideas, new brands, and new products—everything moves a lot, and we've faced many challenges. The way we manage is through Channel Op's ability to forecast a year in advance. In the first meeting we had with Tyler, he said, "You're going to reach $50,000 by the end of this year." Then, we did. In the meeting after we hit our goal, he said, "You're going to reach $100,000 by the end of this year." From there, we've only seen steady growth and accurate predictions year after year.

Really, it's fun trying to understand the consumer and meet their needs via Amazon. As a manager, I lead by example, and sometimes that involves working harder and longer. With all of that pressure on you, how you handle stressful situations is very important. With Channel Op, you can see how every employee manages their stress well, even in a fast-paced, constantly changing industry. Tyler knows where he and his clients are going, and it's a straight line-up.

All Good: The History of Channel Op's Pricing Model

For the first few years of running Channel Op, we didn't have a monthly minimum; we just took a percentage of sales. We worked with some great brands, but sometimes those brands were really small with that percentage being under $200 a month. Over time, we've had to make the choice of raising our monthly minimum, mostly because I wanted to compensate my employees better. As a result, we've lost some clients with each raise. I always hate that because I want to see the best outcomes for every brand we take on. Though, even with our monthly minimum, we're often the most affordable option, especially when one of the alternatives is a brand building its own internal Amazon department from the ground up. Not to mention, we do great work and provide a whole lot more stability; with Channel Op, there's never a day where a brand's account is neglected.

Before instilling our monthly minimum requirement, Channel Op also featured tiered pricing. If a brand sold more than $50,000 a month, I would offer a discount on the percentage Channel Op claimed. For their first two years with Channel Op, All Good, an eco-friendly sunscreen brand that has been with me since the beginning, made that $50,000 their sales goal. When I first approached their vice president of sales and marketing, Ryan Rich, I never expected to see them grow at such a quick rate. At one time, the $50,000 goal seemed ambitious, but in the last three years, All Good has blown that objective out of the water. Their secret? All Good maintains a real-deal kind of partnership with Channel Op. They nail their operations outside of Amazon, and they trust us to uphold the same level of efficiency and expertise when managing their product page.

On top of prioritizing Amazon and keeping a collaboration-centric mindset, All Good is also extremely adept at evolving product offerings. An early version of All Good's sunscreen contained zinc and did not rub into the skin as well as their current products. Customers began leaving reviews on their Amazon page, attaching images of white stripes of sunscreen across people's arms and legs. All Good's executives did not shirk away from this feedback, however; they embraced it and skillfully pivoted to developing a new formula. Then, when they rolled out the new version, they trusted Channel Op to transfer the sales numbers from the old Amazon listing to the new one, update the product titles, and garner better feedback. Their constant experimentation not only helps Channel Op do its job well, but it also enables them to continue being a really good company filled with really good people who are working towards a really good mission: offering more sustainable, cruelty-free skincare products for all.

All Good: Ryan Rich, Vice President of Sales and Marketing[2]

When Tyler first approached me, Amazon was still in its infant years. No one knew how the website, or eCommerce in general, would evolve in the next decade, but as the head of sales for All Good, I'm always looking for the next big growth opportunity. Amazon seemed like a way to expand our brand presence. However, back in the day, retailers were not huge fans of companies selling on Amazon for a variety of reasons, so All Good planned to have Amazon sales only take up a small percentage of the business. The only problem was that we had no idea where to even start with the platform. We had tried to set up our own product page ourselves, only to give up after 48 hours of working on it. The task seemed like a total joke and nightmare wrapped into one. With Tyler's card in my hand, I knew I needed to call him.

When I enlisted Channel Op's help, I had no idea that Amazon would become our biggest customer. I mean, I look at numbers all day long, so when I see our sales increasing day by day and doubling year by year, I just say, "Let's keep it going." My wife, Caroline Duell, is the CEO of All Good, and as a B-corporation leader, she stands for using business as a force of good. She has built integrity into the DNA of All Good. We operate with a triple bottom line in mind: take care of your workers, take care of the planet, and take care of your profits. The revenue stream we gain from Amazon empowers us to maintain the morals our company was founded on.

My background is in organic farming, and Caroline's background is in wilderness medicine and mountaineering. All Good began on a farm in California when Caroline started making a balm from a garden she planted. I used it to heal the cracks in my hands from farming, and she used it to mend her beaten-up hands from rock climbing. The balm was good for everything; it was our hero product. So, we called it "All Good Goop" and began selling it at local farmer's markets. I joined my wife two years after she started the company as her sales guy, and fast forward to present day, we are an environmentally-forward, organic sunscreen brand that's moving into bigger selling spaces, such as Target and Kroger. Our digital presence is almost half of our entire business, and that includes Amazon.

Kim Lynch has been All Good's brand manager for years now. I always look at it like if the president of the company is still managing our brand, then we must be pretty good customers. I'll be transparent: All Good is bombarded by multiple Amazon management agencies every year, and I've taken the time to look over a couple of their portfolios. After considering their services, I can honestly say that I believe Channel Op has the most diverse selection of offerings out of any other agency. I've never seen another company that provides what Channel Op provides, especially when you consider their hands-on approach, advertising management, and forecasting services. Plus, I've yet to find anyone else who is more relationship-driven.

There are always challenges in business, right? The same is true with our Amazon product page. We've had our fair share of complications, especially with how COVID-19 impacted shipment rates, but these roadblocks are always solved through extremely candid, honest conversations with Tyler and the Channel Op team. For Tyler to see me at a trade show and ask me to sit down with him for a beer, not to sell me on anything but just to talk business, goes above and beyond the conversations I typically have with other agencies. In our current era of business, where it's difficult to predict what your level of growth will look like in the next couple of years due to global catastrophe after global catastrophe, it's critical to have a team on your side that is as dedicated

> as you are to launching more products and kicking up the pace for Amazon growth.

Everyone at Channel Op cherishes the relationships with the brands we work with. Each account has its own challenges unique to the brand, and we're excited to tackle them for businesses of all sizes. While we look forward to helping smaller brands on Amazon put their best foot forward, we also cater to larger brands with a diverse range of products that want to continue expanding their Amazon presence. Every company has its own story about how it started and grew into its current state; Channel Op exists as a part of that story, guiding brands along their Amazon journey and building a better experience for both the brand and its customers.

— CHAPTER 4 —
EMPLOYEE
EXPERIENCE

Every entrepreneur knows what it's like working *in* your business rather than *on* your business when you start out. When Channel Op first got its legs, I performed every task by myself. I was the face of the company and worked with every brand on a personal level. As the company grew and more employees joined the team, though, I quickly realized how my all-encompassing role wasn't as helpful anymore. In fact, I was hindering the progress of my company in some ways. Relinquishing control as your company grows, I discovered, is hard to do but necessary. Adding more members to your team requires a level of trust, which means believing they can handle all of the responsibilities that were once yours. It's a cyclical process of accepting duties as the proud CEO, learning that you are the bottleneck, and then figuring out how to pull yourself back without hurting your ego. I used to be the best at everything; now I have a team that's better than me at everything.

This team-building process informed Channel Op's company culture. Channel Op is an agency that services other businesses with a certain set of expectations for high-level services and outcomes. Our team understands that we are helping companies manage between a third to half of their total revenue; Amazon is a massive channel. However, this doesn't mean the job is so serious that my team and I can't come together to do something fun every once in a while. We aren't packing foosball and ping-pong tables into the office like some cliché startups, but some off-site get-togethers every now and then help the team members become better collaborators. Then, when an employee needs to ask for help, they are a little more comfortable and willing to approach a coworker. If you're not cognizant of your team's morale and comfort levels, no single mission statement or slogan will save the day.

Channel Op's president, Kim Lynch, acts as the glue that fosters this open communication and positivity. Looking back, Kim has always been a source of stability and organization in the once-chaotic startup environment that I often refer to as our "wild west" days. On one of her first shifts with Channel Op, I took Kim and a couple of other newly appointed brand managers to Outdoor Retailer Expo, a popular convention full of professionals cutting loose and having a drink or two. Amidst the drinking, chatting, and good-time-having, Kim broke apart from our group, walked the sales floor, and tested her pitch for selling Channel Op's services. At this point, she barely knew what Channel Op was even selling, let alone the branding language we used to market ourselves. But there she was, talking to big-hitter clients and maintaining a professional air from day one.

As she underwent training and took on projects for herself, she became very strategic in how she approached me with project updates or ideas. She always had a high level of emotional intelligence that she used to facilitate productive conversations between teammates and pitch process improvement suggestions to me. Before long, I promoted her from brand manager to senior brand manager, but I quickly realized that her people skills would be better suited to management. So, she adopted the title of director of operations before climbing the ladder to president in a short period. Kim is now a trusted beacon of hope within our company; no one hesitates to speak to her if they have an issue or need extra support. I wish I could take credit for her achievements and say that her success directly stemmed from my training, but the fact is that I had nothing to do with her development. Kim became an integral part of Channel Op by relying on her own merit, abilities, and work ethic. That, among other factors, is what makes Channel Op stand out—all of our leaders are homegrown.

Kim Lynch, President[3]

When I interviewed for a position at Channel Op, the company didn't have its own office, instead operating out of a co-working space. Stepping into the doors, I initially felt a welcoming vibe from the team. Tyler and the rest of the company, which was small at the time, were sipping on mimosas and celebrating a recent win. I remember feeling very comfortable during my one-on-one interview with Tyler. He was straightforward and direct, but he held an obvious passion for his company, using the whiteboard in the room to explain his plans for taking Channel Op to the next level.

I was initially hired as a brand manager, and then I adopted a role as a senior brand manager before moving to my previous role as director of operations. I was excited to move into the director of operations role so that I could work on advancing Channel Op's operational procedures, especially the training process as it was nonexistent at the

---

time. Throughout my career, I've always had a knack for standardizing processes and asking, "How can we improve? What can we do better?"

Although process development came easily, I found myself in a major leadership role for the first time in my career. Scheduling, directing, and leading meetings became a necessity, a task that seemed intimidating for a natural introvert like myself. I was forced to break out of my shell and accept the challenge. Plus, as I worked to take on these new leadership duties, Tyler hesitated to relinquish his, making for an interesting dynamic in the early days. Tyler had his hands in every facet of Channel Op; enabling him to take a step back from some of his responsibilities would be the only way for the company to progress.

Tyler and I found a dynamic that works, interestingly enough, by using the same whiteboard he used during my first interview. Watching how he interacted with other employees, I found that many would always agree with him, no matter what he proposed. More than anything, Tyler needed some pushback on his ideas, someone to play devil's advocate. When both of us would stay late into the evenings, I would ask for his thoughts on a process improvement idea or another thought he'd had that day. Then, we'd bounce ideas back and forth, using the whiteboard to jot down notes. To this day, I think that if someone were to sit in on one of those meetings, they'd come away thinking, "Wow, those two people are not on the same page at all." In reality, we adopt different leadership approaches that balance each other out and strengthen Channel Op's ability to innovate.

Independence as an Amazon Brand Manager

Currently, we have a 36-person team of brand managers, each working with six to 10 clients. When we're looking for those key brand manager characteristics, we hire based on a range of skills. Communication is key as it defines the relationship with clients. We work with C-suite executives to warehouse managers, so the ability to meet someone at their level while being clear and concise is important. Managers are expected to have a high level of attention to detail as there are plenty of small aspects of Amazon that need to be monitored. If an employee doesn't know something or is unsure, that's okay. We don't expect everyone to know everything. It's a willingness to ask for help that makes a truly successful member of our team. New team members are encouraged to ask questions, especially during those first three weeks of formal training. Usually, after three months, they are ready to take on clients. Nine months in, they're comfortable and fully integrated but still remain willing to ask anyone on the team for help.

There's something special about managing the managers. I am always in favor of choosing to trust the employee over micromanaging them. Managers—

and really, every employee on the team—work rather independently, making decisions without entirely relying on outside guidance. One big reason for this is there just isn't enough time to micromanage someone else. We are a small team; it would be a waste of resources. This level of freedom allows managers to try new things, work at their own pace, and define their own schedules. Channel Op can teach a manager how to be successful on Amazon, but we can't teach them how to be organized. It doesn't come down to the hours put in, but the results from all the work.

Whenever I think of a Channel Op team member taking initiative, I think of our current manager of brand success, Michelle Brandon. Michelle started at Channel Op as my executive assistant, and though she never adopted the role of brand manager, she worked her way up to a leadership role, overseeing how our brand managers operate. Her personal growth is likely one of the most impressive out of any employee I've ever hired. As my executive assistant, Michelle managed my calendar, helped with email correspondence, and scheduled sales calls—basic assistant tasks. I'd only assign her around six to eight hours of work per week, not anywhere near enough to fill a full-time position. Despite this, she'd find other work to fill in the remaining 30 or so hours. Once, she came to me and said, "We don't have an employee handbook, so I'm going to write one." After recognizing she wasn't qualified to perform certain HR tasks, she approached me and asked, "Can I spend time studying to pass an HR certification exam?" I even remember expressing my desire to have a notary in the office, and low and behold, Michelle went and obtained a notary license soon after.

Michelle has always been someone who wants more out of her career. Trying to find a position that enabled her to perform more important tasks, she briefly left Channel Op for larger companies. She gained some experience with them and learned more about how an established business operates, and deciding that she didn't want to spend the rest of her life restocking mini-fridges and scheduling phone calls, she returned to Channel Op and expressed her desire to accept more responsibility. She is now our manager of operations, meaning that on top of onboarding new clients, hiring new employees, and handling HR needs, Michelle is Channel Op's very own problem-solving aficionado. She continues to excel in her role as a proactive leader, acting as a vital resource for those around her. I wish I could say that, as a seasoned leader, I was single-handedly responsible for Michelle's evolution, but the truth is that Michelle took it upon herself not only to want more but to actively strive for more. She is the perfect example of someone who flourishes in Channel Op's culture—an independent, eager go-getter who works toward achieving their professional goals.

Michelle Brandon, Manager of Brand Success[4]

I first started at Channel Op as Tyler's executive assistant, though I never felt like I was only there to assist him. Tyler has always been someone who can see the potential in people and lets them pursue any plans or objectives they have.

I was always given a seat at the table. Now, as Channel Op's manager of brand success, I have the privilege of giving other people leadership responsibilities and seeing how they run with it, too.

Over the span of my career, I've had the opportunity to work for a couple of other larger companies in various roles. Supporting these companies' executive leadership teams not only taught me how a multi-million-dollar organization operates, but also that I wanted more for my career. I'm not someone who can sit on the sidelines while the higher-ups handle the specialized work. I believe I have a talent for finding ways to improve processes and procedures while elevating the responsibilities of my role in the company. Tyler is one of the only bosses I've had who has let me spread my wings and empowered me to make real changes that I can still see reflected in the company today.

Channel Op has a special recipe for building leaders. Our leaders do not micromanage; they trust our staff to find the answers themselves and really take ownership of their brands and projects. If I've learned anything as the manager responsible for onboarding new hires, rockstar employees—and the employees who tend to gain the most from their time at Channel Op—enjoy learning and self-discovery. They don't settle for mediocrity or "good enough." They figure out how to cook with the key ingredients Channel Op provides. These are the people who build lasting connections and relationships with their brands and coworkers. They have a passion in and out of the business, and they don't sweat the small stuff, which is great because, honestly, that's how Amazon eats you alive.

eCommerce is obviously not going anywhere anytime soon as anyone can see from how much Amazon's presence has grown in the past couple of years. Now, if a brand isn't on Amazon, customers ask, "Why?" Even as Amazon continues to change, roll out new features, and update policies, Channel Op grows with it. Our company is in a unique position right now where everyone is focused on growth and building the infrastructure to support our upward mobility. Our success will come from where it's always come from: providing our team with the support, direction, and independence it needs to progress right alongside the constantly developing Amazon landscape.

The Daily Brand Manager Grind

Various Amazon tools define a brand's online presence, meaning that managing a brand's product page requires constant attention. SKUs are at the forefront of inventory management, but clicks need to be counted as part of the advertising numbers, not to mention all the other ad hoc tasks that make their way to a brand manager's desk. Our managers have to be pretty adept at organization since schedules require day-to-day attention as well as overarching week-to-week planning. On top of that expected grind, Amazon has a tendency to just "break" on its own as the website changes settings and formats, which can shift bullet points on product pages or stop images from loading. Brand managers are ready to jump on those problems as they pop up, putting out fires before Amazon customers and clients can even notice anything has gone wrong.

When making larger management decisions, we work hand in hand with clients to make sure their brand's Amazon presence is beyond what they can envision. However, it takes time to collect and analyze all of the data we handle, informing those strategic choices that build our week-to-week plans. For example, going through the search volume for keywords to explore new advertising targets takes time. Once brand managers have a plan for coming up with innovative new approaches for product listings, they'll communicate it to clients and then act on it once everyone's on the same page. Managers at Channel Op are all versatile, each with their own special Amazon abilities. A brand's main category on Amazon starts to matter when writing copy (titles, bullets, keywords, etc.). It's a blend of science and art for brand managers to find that balance between the most-used keywords and an enticing, understandable title. Even with the surplus of data we can utilize, the client experience is the real measure of success for us.

If communication between managers and the client has been infrequent but sales are up 25%, the win won't matter unless the client feels heard. At the end of the day, brands should feel in control of their Amazon page;

Channel Op's goal is to fuel their success. As someone who has managed many brands, I can confirm there is a certain satisfaction that comes with helping a client succeed. I've had clients come in and start selling $5,000 a month, only for us to boost their revenue to $50,000 a month. We've had brand owners tell managers Channel Op has enabled them to start finally paying themselves or hiring new employees. We understand that behind every brand, there are real people looking to start or grow their businesses. Channel Op continues to grow alongside them, and this only fuels our motivation. New and interesting work presents itself every day with our employees leading the way through Amazon's constantly expanding landscape.

Our brand managers don't tackle all of this on their own, though; we thrive on the collaboration between our U.S.-based managers and our support teams in the Philippines. Channel Op's success is owed to the abilities and dedication of employees spread across the world, working towards making brands' goals into realities.

CHAPTER 5

THE
PHILIPPINES

Due to the constraints of remote work, the COVID-19 pandemic significantly impacted my team in the Philippines. They felt accustomed to working together in their main office where they had access to computers and in-person camaraderie. From their own homes, work became more of a struggle against technology and isolation.

In May of 2022, I traveled to Manila, bringing as many laptops, monitors, and keyboards as I could check onto the airplane. I'm not a seasoned international traveler by any means, so enduring the long, 40-hour flight meant that after a certain point, I had to give up on any sense of normalcy. By the end of the journey, a few of the monitors had broken during transit, but nonetheless, the Philippines team greatly appreciated the new gear. I spent the week talking to the team one-on-one and taking stock of everyone's well-being. My visit was colored by the care and attention to detail that Ava Castro, our director of operations in the Philippines, brings to every project. She planned my entire visit: cars were available to transport people, food and drink were prepared in advance—every single box was checked. The entire team and I were able to celebrate without any unexpected problems or delays, dancing, joking, and talking well into the night.

Being the boss from thousands of miles away comes with a significant downside: leadership can feel impersonal and cold. The world had drastically changed since my last trip to Manila in 2019, so I saw an opportunity to introduce myself to new employees I hadn't met in person and establish stronger bonds with employees who have been with Channel Op for years. When I make the effort to come to the Philippines, I can become a real human being in my team's eyes rather than just another Slack message requiring a response.

I was first introduced to the idea of hiring assistants in the Philippines while working with River Runners. We were a small team of five, and three of those positions were temps. Their turnover rate was high, most of them being ski bums from Park City, so I was frustrated with our overall employee situation. Managing them soaked up so much of my time that I couldn't even focus on how to make them productive. As I was thinking of leaving River Runners and starting my own company, an acquaintance from the trade shows we frequented sent out an email letting me know about their friend who was starting an eCommerce outsourcing company in the Philippines. I was desperate for any help I could get, so I took the risk and reached out.

They were a tiny company composed of just the CEO and three employees. I had them start out with some really small, simple tasks. I had a client with over 200 toy SKUs, and I needed to have the titles, bullets, and images reviewed. The assistants in the Philippines did a high-quality, quick job, and they did it better than the U.S. team. Incredibly happy with their work, I reached back out to the eCommerce outsourcing company when I left River Runners. April was the first full-time person I hired through them, and she was an absolutely killer rockstar. From there, I just kept building the team, and after a year, I was by far their fastest-growing client: I had six people in the U.S. and 10 people in the Philippines.

Empowerment in Outsourcing

The work Channel Op requires from the Philippines team differs from most outsourcing work. I came to learn that many of the other teams working within the recruiting company were focused on customer service, which mostly entailed answering non-stop phone calls. My team's work was mostly ticket-based Amazon tasks and document reviews, so they had the freedom to joke around within a more natural work environment instead of gluing themselves to a phone. The collaborative team dynamic built up a real sense of comradery, and the U.S. team works to make sure the Philippines team feels like a vital part of the company, sending them company shirts, gifts, and other tokens of appreciation. I've been told on multiple occasions that this is different from how other clients at the outsourcing company have treated them in the past.

Some people unfortunately see outsourcing as a necessary evil that involves giving unwanted tasks to "less-than" workers. I find this to be a disrespectful approach to management because it removes the humanity that is so clearly a business advantage. It also ignores basic human decency. Everyone is working towards the same goal, and I need every member of the team; otherwise, I wouldn't have hired them.

Our backend team in the Philippines deserves all the support we can give them. They are able to handle any task that comes their way, as well as any error Amazon throws at them. Amazon will shut down product listings for a range of reasons, but the Philippines branch is able to identify, document, and resolve problems as quickly as possible. A large part of that is their ability to contact Amazon's Seller Support with the right nuances. Amazon's support channel only has so many people handling cases, so highlighting problems and underlining the proper phrases ensures a response that isn't a simple template message. Our team has become so adept at resolving problems that a product could be taken down and then relisted within a day. For someone who manages their own Amazon accounts, the same process could take up to two weeks. The Philippines team handles these issues so efficiently; you can imagine how their work takes a massive load off of the U.S. team.

A productive workflow is only possible through proper communication between the Philippines and U.S. offices. The Philippines branch is able to process our internal reports that we use for making decisions about accounts on an ad hoc or scheduled basis. With the Philippines team starting their day in a time zone before the U.S. team, the brand managers can come into the office with all of their reports built out and waiting for them. The communication carries over to clients as well. If a client has 100 SKUs and decides to execute a rebranding, we now have 100 new products that we have to rebrand, which requires new images, logos, and wording. The brand manager and clients will make those decisions, but someone in the Philippines will be the one who executes them. We'll make sure that the Philippines team member is on the initial call with the client, taking notes. Clear division of duties and open communication allow Channel Op to support all of the brands and their needs.

I think a large amount of the success of the Philippines branch lies in the amount of ownership we give them. I've hired so many amazing people there and had such little turnover; my employees know that we care and listen. Their opinions and the opinions of our U.S. team are treated with equal weight. I think that matters way more than people realize. Letting someone have a voice and then seeing how their thoughts made a lasting change is incredibly empowering. I shy away from micromanagement whenever I can, but it's physically impossible for me to look over anyone's shoulder when I'm more than 7,000 miles away. Still, I trust the teams and their leadership to manage themselves. We've created an infrastructure where employees can feel supported in their work and encouraged to invest in making their job—and their teammates' jobs—better.

Leadership in the Philippines

Creating an organization that remains strong while being divided between two countries has been somewhat of a learning curve for me as a leader, and it has required a lot of experimentation. For example, all of our employees initially only adopted one of two roles: U.S. brand manager or Philippines brand assistant. Now, however, the multiple departments within the Philippines branch act as a network of specialty groups that support the U.S. brand managers. Building out these two roles into multiple positions meant reverting the U.S. side to just brand managers and diversifying the departments in the Philippines. Ava, the director of operations in the Philippines, oversees the four departments under her:

assistant brand managers, creative, advertising, and channel control. My experiments with other departments didn't necessarily work every time. At one point, there was a customer service department that lost relevance when Amazon took away the ability to reply to negative reviews. There was also a reimbursements team that ended up not needing specialization as assistant brand managers were able to perform this role as part of their duties.

There would be no room for experimentation without the leadership of Ava, though. She started as an assistant and worked her way up to the director of operations position, and she has proven herself every step of the way. Promoting employees purely based on their performance makes a lot of sense, but the strengths they have in one role may also hold them back at the next level. Promoting to management is an especially gray area as it is difficult to go from receiving directions to directing others. I can confidently say that despite this risk, Ava has thrived in every single promotion she's received, working with minimal oversight and achieving maximum results.

As we've formalized each department, we've even tried to optimize teams around her. Channel Op's turnover rate in the Philippines is extremely low thanks to Ava's ability to treat everyone with the respect they deserve. She is so adept at listening and making her team feel heard. It's rare for us to lose team members because Ava understands that I see the Phillippines team as just as important as the U.S. team. Without them—and without Ava—Channel Op doesn't work.

When Tyler first interviewed me for the position of eCommerce Specialist, I was more shy than I am now and not as confident in my English-speaking skills. I remember him asking me about how my day was, my past work experience, and how good I am with Excel. It wasn't like any job interview I'd ever had before, yet my nervousness seemed to melt away as we talked. Tyler pulled the confidence out of me for the discussion, and after some time had passed, I began working at Channel Op as an assistant to Kim Lynch, who is now our company's president. Kim provided me with all of the leadership skills I needed to grow in my role and perform my duties well. From my perspective, it's no wonder Kim has moved to such a high position in the company.

In my first role, I worked hard. I worked really hard. Still, I didn't expect my promotions from eCommerce specialist to junior team leader to senior team leader and then finally to my current position, director of operations for the Philippines team. I attribute a lot of my success to Kim for giving me such valuable tools, but I have also grown as a leader myself since joining Channel Op. My leadership style prioritizes my relationships with others and open conversation. I don't consider myself the boss; I just want everyone to feel comfortable reaching out to me and honestly expressing themselves. The Philippines team is centered on positivity and kindness, and at the end of the day, everything comes down to trust between me and my team.

Managing a department that is so far away from its parent company does have its own unique set of challenges, though, especially now that the Philippines team has transitioned to a completely remote working environment. Working in person allows a team to build a certain type of bond, and I miss that in our current virtual space. As we're all very close here in the Philippines, we now facilitate team dinners once a month and play online games together at the end of each week to prevent any kind of disconnect.

Our business environment can best be described as fun and loud with some light teasing thrown in. At the same time, there are some cultural differences between the Philippines and U.S. teams. My team members tend to ask me, "Is Tyler mad?" after they receive Slack messages from him. This isn't because Tyler is actually angry, but because Tyler is a straightforward person, and online messages don't allow for many expression. All of their hesitance vanishes once Tyler visits the Philippines and the team can interact with him in person, though. This last time, any newcomers who hadn't met Tyler in person went from anxious to dancing with him for TikTok videos. I remember staying up with Tyler and the team until 3 am that night, just talking and enjoying each other's company.

The Philippines team is a unique part of Channel Op, but it's also the company's backbone. While the brand managers directly work with clients, we build, protect, and create value for each individual brand from the sidelines, and we always make sure to give our 100% when providing the best level of service. Ever since I left my role as an eCommerce specialist, the position has grown to adopt so many new and important responsibilities. Our knowledge is constantly evolving, and there are always new opportunities for learning on the horizon.

The Philippines team now acts as an integral part of Channel Op, and the team's impressive growth means we must now restructure the company to fully incorporate each employee. Hiring a third-party outsourcing company worked well in our beginning stages, but now, the Philippines team has achieved self-sustainability. In addition, working through a third party means that even though my brand assistants worked for Channel Op, I still technically remained a client of this outsourcing company. My ultimate objective with the Philippines team is to make them feel like they are part of Channel Op. Going forward, the way to foster that loyalty and sense of belonging is to employ the team directly. Many companies would then hire them as contractors as a solution, but doing so leaves them responsible for their own taxes and health insurance. The fear of being fired at any moment as an independent contractor doesn't build a foundation. When you pay someone as a contractor, they will not be able to qualify for loans, apply for a mortgage, or build a life of their own. I want everyone on the Philippines team to know that I have their back; it's vital they understand that they have 100% of Channel Op's support.

To actually offer up that support, Channel Op has begun forming a company in the Philippines. The costs of creating a company there are negligible compared to the possibility of hurting retention and morale. When making this decision, I considered every possible angle, asking myself, "Would I hire my U.S. employees as independent contractors or cut some other corners to work around the third-party company?" My answer came easily to me: of course not. So, why would I turn around and do that to my employees in the Philippines? Turns out, I wouldn't— because everyone at Channel Op deserves the respect that comes from producing great work.

CHAPTER 6

THE IMPACT
OF COVID-19

There are no positives to how COVID-19 changed the world, and I can't stress that enough. However, the pandemic did push people to shop online, which absolutely favored Amazon. We saw Amazon integrate even more into our everyday infrastructure, bringing packages straight to our doorsteps when we couldn't leave our homes. Brick-and-mortar stores simply weren't an option, and online brands took advantage of this. Channel Op brands didn't see a 200% increase in profits like Amazon did,[6] but overall, they had about a 10-20% increase in sales. The growth wasn't inherent, though; it required a level of flexibility and patience many weren't used to.

I watched brands adapt to the needs of consumers in clever ways. Some of the beauty product brands Channel Op manages stopped production of their normal products to manufacture hand sanitizers. Channel Op didn't directly benefit from this as Amazon established many regulations and hoops to jump through for selling hand sanitizer, but the experience did show that businesses were keyed into consumer needs. Businesses were not the only group that changed their habits, however. With the state of the economy at the time, shoppers became especially thoughtful with how they spent their hard-earned money.

By March 2021, stimulus spending had produced an uptick in sales, but it didn't last forever. A year later, the world became more accessible—people could enter public spaces and re-explore their favorite stores.[7] With the inflation of 2022, the bare necessities of housing and food became much more expensive, eating into the public's ability to spend. Overall, there has been a softening in eCommerce, most likely the rightsizing from a drop in demand. I wouldn't call it a slip back to the way things were before, but the tap has been tightened on the once-overflowing marketplace. With all of the numbers that the pandemic affected, we have to remember there were real human consequences, even at Channel Op.

The New Remote Work Environment

The part of the business most affected by COVID-19 was the workplace setting. From 2015 to 2020, the Channel Op U.S. team would commonly work in the office for four days out of the week and spend one day at home. We were a small team, but our camaraderie greatly benefited from sharing that space together. As an eternal optimist, I assured the team at the start of the pandemic, "We'll probably be back at the office in two or three weeks." I kept repeating this every few weeks, hoping we would be able to return to our office in Park City, but that day never came. Channel Op had used co-working spaces and the public library before leasing our office; unfortunately, the need to stay at home forced us to terminate the lease. When it came time to transition to a fully remote work environment, the U.S. team already had decent work setups in their homes. This was not the case with our Philippines team.

Pre-COVID, the Philippines team worked in the office, five days a week. Many worked on desktop computers in the office, so they didn't have laptops when our company converted to a remote workplace. I took it upon myself to deliver laptops, monitors, and keyboards to Manila not only to supply my team with the necessary equipment but also to show them that, even in the midst of a difficult pandemic, there was still someone on their side. With the entire world in disarray, I wanted them to know their jobs were safe and their work was appreciated.

Morale was especially difficult to maintain, especially with video conferencing and phone calls as our main sources of communication. When working in the U.S. office, my team and I engaged in many simple activities to sustain morale, such as eating lunch as a team or visiting an escape room together. Once COVID hit, we had to severely limit these in-person interactions outside of work. Suddenly not seeing your coworkers, especially if they are your friends, makes for a sad transition. Our work and home lives melded into one, and it came at a cost. Burnout became more of a risk, so I made sure my employees took mental health days for themselves. Many Channel Op team members, myself included, struggled to adapt to this new lifestyle.

In fact, to be quite frank, I feel like I was the least ready for it. I was not prepared to remotely manage full-time. In person, I could better understand my team members' feelings and workload. Picking up on tone over a Slack message is difficult, and without body language, my direct approach to communication doesn't tend to translate well. I now have to clearly state to new hires that, whenever I message them about a problem, I am only interested in solving the problem. I never wish to comment on their ability or work performance in an off-handed way. Working alongside these new teammates in an office, I could have personable moments passing them in the hall, but with my completely electronic messages, managing morale became an unforeseen challenge. Over time, I've developed a new skill: balancing communication with team members between goal-oriented work messages and more general conversational interactions.

The Pandemic's Effects on Brand Management

Channel Op also had to modify our communication tactics with brands. The pandemic created a fog of uncertainty that permeated how our brands operated overnight. Clients stopped making decisions as if they were in limbo, fearful of what the future might hold. Would they even have jobs in three months? In one month? Luckily, everyone seemed to sustain their careers, but from March to September 2020, brands moved much slower and more cautiously. It was even difficult to start conversations with salespeople, let alone close a deal.

Trade shows are an important space for us to pursue new clients and maintain relationships with current clients. COVID-19 made these spaces unviable; traveling for work was not an option. Closing sales is always easier in person, but we were forced to work purely over email and phone calls. I can sign clients remotely, but there is something meaningful about looking someone in the eye and saying, "Hey, we can really do this job for you." A relationship built in person cannot be replaced. A brand's Amazon presence can make up a third to half of its total company revenue, so who manages this revenue is a big decision. Without the proper trust established from the beginning, the choice can result in major repercussions. The pandemic certainly impacted the way Channel Op found and onboarded new clients, but as we all know, COVID affected all areas of life—and consequently, all areas of business—in ways that still linger to this day, especially with the supply chain.

In 2021, "the failing supply chain" was on everyone's lips as their packages took longer to arrive. Even though supply chain issues had not affected the rest of the world yet, they became a problem as soon as 2020. The moment COVID hit and sales on Amazon started exceeding normal levels, Amazon placed many restrictions on inbound SKUs to their warehouse shipping. Our standard process of stocking up brands involves having eight or more weeks' worth of inventory in an Amazon warehouse at a time. The availability in the warehouses began to shrink as other sellers shipped in extra inventory and demand skyrocketed. It became a real fight for inventory storage.

Around April 2020, we had a truckload of sandals already packed up at our client's warehouse, waiting for the truck to transport it to Amazon's warehouse. While the truck waited on the shipping dock, Amazon made a change to their algorithm, restricting the number of units that could be shipped into their warehouses. This client's prime season for sandals sales in May, June, and July, so this stock-up delivery was essential to prepare for the summer season. Once we realized the delivery had halted, another employee and I sat on the phone for hours to ensure the 50,000 units of sandals went through. If we didn't succeed, we would lose out on at least $3 million in sales. Working with the client, we finally reached the Amazon representative who could authorize the shipment . . . but only because it had been approved before they changed the algorithm. Many other summer-centric clients were not so lucky with their stock-ups, so we had to shift our strategy.

In order to maintain stock amongst all the demand, we scheduled seven or eight shipments every week instead of one large shipment every two weeks, our normal routine. Amazon placed restrictions on accounts as well as individual items, and the company established a schedule for how much inventory you could send in at one time. Any time inventory space was available to us, we filled it up. If they had space for 20,000 units in the warehouse, we would send the 400 units that we could as soon as it opened up. This model of managing inventory greatly stressed our team, whereas before, they had a consistent schedule for stocking. We could maintain this system with our clients, but I know of others who were not as lucky.

A company that I used to work with experienced a real-life horror story during the pandemic. The company exceeded Amazon's allowance for inventory, which meant that, in order to stock new products, the founder had to request the destruction of $200,000 worth of units. He had too much non-moving inventory that was essentially stuck in the Amazon system, and it simply wasn't selling fast enough. While he couldn't stop the sales of his best sellers with this hold-up, he also had nowhere else to store the inventory in Amazon's warehouse. Having it destroyed remained the only option. As Amazon stopped allowing shipments, he then had to furlough his entire warehouse staff of about 30 people. Stories like this weren't uncommon during the first months of the pandemic, and this only exacerbated the fear everyone already had.

That being said, Channel Op was extremely lucky with how adaptable we could be from 2020 to 2022. I felt blessed to keep my employees by transitioning to a remote work environment, while many others had to work with bureaucracies and governments to figure out what came next for their employees and industry. I'm eternally grateful for where Channel Op stands today. In part, the dedication and teamwork of both the U.S. and Philippines teams have enabled us to be as successful as we were during the pandemic.

Today, that success is only continuing to grow. Amazon's future has been further cemented by the influx of sales over the pandemic, and Channel Op will continue to navigate working on the world's largest eCommerce platform. The brands we work with are diverse and widespread, and we'll continue exploring how to help them progress on Amazon.

CHAPTER 7

THE FUTURE OF AMAZON ALONGSIDE CHANNEL OP

When looking to the future, people often ask, "What is the next Amazon?" Sorry, but there is no next Amazon... at least, for now. They have made themselves indispensable in our modern infrastructure with their incredible advantage in logistics. As of 2021, their warehouses cover about 319 million square feet in the U.S. alone.[8] They have the necessary planes and trucks to move inventory across the entire world, competing with UPS and FedEx. Yes, they are an eCommerce site, but their systems have expanded to become so much more.

Even competitors attempting to copy Amazon's models, such as Walmart, can't possibly catch up. Walmart is trillions of dollars behind Amazon in replicating its infrastructure; they simply don't have the amount of money necessary to surpass its main competitor. Walmart has worked off of the hub and spoke model, utilizing a hub warehouse to serve their surrounding stores. Unlike Amazon, Walmart has not adapted to serving individual customers. Their infrastructure is built around a B2B network rather than Amazon's B2C network.

Walmart currently has the upper-hand in managing its brick-and-mortar locations. Amazon matches its competition with grocery products, though; the company didn't even have to build the infrastructure by itself to do it. When they wanted to expand into groceries, they acquired Whole Foods, quickly catching up with competitors to have skin in the game. In the same way that Amazon bought Whole Foods and Zappos, I could see them also acquiring a customer-centric clothing retailer like Nordstroms and further extending into the fashion market. They have the ability to keep expanding in every direction. No one else is like Amazon, and the years of 2020 and 2021 prove that.

COVID-19's effect on Amazon has been a once-in-a-lifetime catalyst for its growth, but this growth has been an upward trend for some time, especially with its advertising arm. No other eCommerce site also plays a role as one of the largest players in the online advertising marketplace. In 2018, Amazon Advertising generated $10 billion. By 2021, Amazon's $31.6 billion ad revenue surpassed Youtube's $28.8 billion revenue from the same year, although this number is still below Google's $69.4 billion.[9] That being said, when Amazon is the starting point for so many customer journeys, the necessity to be seen first amongst competitors has never been more important.

Amazon remains the most cost-efficient platform for advertising against Facebook and Google because of their buyers' mindsets. Amazon is a channel to buy products, so the audience inherently considers making a purchase when they visit the site. The buyers' mindset is not interrupted while engaging with the site, whereas Facebook and Google open the buyer to other distractions, such as videos, links, news articles, and posts from family and friends. Facebook and Google gain clicks if the content appears interesting, not necessarily if the audience intends to buy a product. Though Amazon seems like one of the most optimal platforms for eCommerce in comparison to these other sites, not everyone can take advantage of the marketplace.

Amazon: The Past, Present, and Future

Launching on Amazon has become increasingly more difficult over the past decade. Gone are the days when you could launch a product with a little bit of money set aside for advertising and still reach moderate success. Highly reviewed brands hold the top positions in each category, so making your presence initially known requires more effort than before and can be disheartening for brands that don't have an extensive advertising budget.

As launching a brand has become more resource intensive on Amazon, many looking to make money on the platform have turned to an aggregator business model. Rising to popularity in 2020, aggregators are companies that began raising capital and buying up Amazon-centric brands to create a portfolio of already profitable products. These companies buy third-party Amazon sellers with lower multiples, increasing the valuations to six to 10 times their original multiples by the end of their purchasing sprees. Not only do aggregators arbitrage multiples, but they also have revenue from day one as all these businesses are cash-flow positive when acquired. This doesn't mean they stay positive, though.

Some recent industry fallout raises questions about if the aggregator model is sustainable. These companies built their brands around 2020 and 2021 eCommerce data. With numbers boosted by COVID's effect on Amazon, it's unlikely that the same level of revenue can be maintained in the coming years. As COVID enabled these aggregators to raise a surplus of revenue, they have a decent burn amount for the time being, but the need for more funds in the future has the potential to dash their hopes. The amount of venture capital and private equity money has dried up with economic uncertainty. With this occurring at the same time as companies attempting to replicate the aggregator model, the whole situation has the potential to create a bottleneck. Another generation of eCommerce entrepreneurs will inevitably try to become Amazon millionaires, take advantage of the aggregator model, and repeat the process.

Sellers have found that the aggregator model has created an exit plan for many of these small, Amazon-centric brands. There was a stretch of time when anyone could set up a brand on Amazon by buying cheap products on sites like Alibaba. I tend to joke that everyone was buying spatulas and water bottles, but in truth, a substantial amount of kitchenware and water bottle companies started by selling on Amazon. There were even online programs coaching sellers on how to capitalize on the opportunity. Now that aggregators are buying up these niche companies, these quick brand builders have been exiting their companies with significant payout. As more people see these exit strategies succeed, more people will try to establish quick and easy brands on Amazon. The bottleneck will then tighten when the market is flooded with these brands; the more people trying to make money on Amazon, the fewer will succeed.

Even the largest channels need to be more strategic when planning for Amazon's future. Thrasio, one of the biggest aggregators consolidating third-party Amazon sellers, recently had a massive round of layoffs.[10] Thrasio's model worked around their own tech, which was meant to increase profitability in eCommerce operations, but even that, paired with raising billions of dollars in funding, wasn't enough. Pharmapacks, not an aggregator but once one of the top Amazon sellers, filed for bankruptcy in 2022 despite its annual sales exceeding $500 million because the business failed to secure additional financing.[11] Pharmapacks relied on institutional capital rather than revenue, and when its SPAC merger fell through, it didn't stand a chance. Looking at these massive companies, what will it take to maintain success on Amazon?

Long-Term Channel Op Objectives

I think what has helped Channel Op remain successful is the fact that I never raised venture capital and never received equity from a third party. We've never had to spend frivolously, and we've never wanted to. Our business model focuses on our relationships with the brands we work with. Channel Op's brand managers optimize according to goals set by the brands. It's this collaboration, rather than aggregation, that is a signifier for future success. We invest in partnerships with brands and build from there. Our worth isn't dependent on how many companies we can acquire but rather on the work we put into managing brands.

Looking forward, Channel Op is only going to evolve just as Amazon has over the past decades. The first step to that is building up our company in the Philippines. We've taken the necessary steps to integrate the Philippines team into Channel Op's structure. No longer will we rely on an outsourcing company to manage the team; Channel Ops team members will be directly supported as employees. I think this is incredibly important for Channel Op's development because all team members should feel they are growing alongside the company at the same rate.

More than anything, Channel Op is focusing on cementing its company culture. We're setting goals that are both ambitious and attainable. As our teams across the globe collaborate, we are looking for areas to innovate and provide brands with new tools. Channel Op is ready to hire new team members, create new departments, and expand training opportunities. With Kim, Ava, and the rest of our forward-thinking team helping me tackle these big-picture concepts, the future of the company and Amazon looks bright.

Channel Op is looking to grow in new ways as well. We did have recent success acquiring a small agency in 2022 and have retained all of the clients we inherited. I initially had the fear that we would seem like a massive conglomerate compared to the previous agency. The brands might worry they wouldn't gain the same level of attention as before. Unsurprisingly, our teams have stepped up to ensure their brands continue to receive the care they need. Now, I see these clients forming productive bonds with our managers and the rest of Channel Op. Our client base has only grown in diversity, and it fuels the motivation we have for working hard for these brands.

I have seen plenty of brand launches over the history of working on Channel Op. There really is no end to new and exciting products coming to market. Behind all of the small businesses using Amazon as a platform are real people simply trying to get their products in front of consumers. Some massive aggregator isn't funding the launch; it's just someone who has an idea they believe in. My employees have shared with me how fulfilling it is to help support small business owners on their own personal journeys. Running a business, no matter the size, is not easy; it helps to have someone in your corner. Channel Op will continue on its mission to make it easier for brands to launch and grow on the Amazon marketplace while providing a partnership they can believe in.

—— CONCLUSION ——

Around 2018, Channel Op began facilitating quarterly conversations with our brands to plan for the future and provide more strategic support. Before, we helped our clients with more day-to-day or week-to-week issues, and we determined a need for more long-term, holistic solutions and strategies. During these discussions, the conversation often centered around the question: how important is Amazon to the brand's growth? To answer this question, brands began presenting us with sales numbers from their websites, brick-and-mortar stores, and Amazon. Some brands only generated $50,000 in monthly revenue from their website but then saw $250,000 in monthly revenue from Amazon sales. In some cases, a brand's Amazon sales alone surpassed all of its brick-and-mortar sales combined.

This is when the significance of Amazon as an eCommerce platform struck my team and me for the first time. We clearly understood that, yes, we did need to look at the bigger picture and have more overarching conversations with our brands. However, this was not simply to help these brands plan for the future. Rather, the Channel Op team recognized how essential Amazon already was to these brands and knew the platform would only grow to become even more significant.

In one instance, a footwear company presented a PowerPoint to my group, detailing its advertising statistics. Once the company's executives reached the final two slides out of their 20-slide presentation, I realized that the conversion rates on Amazon greatly exceeded the conversion rates from other advertising initiatives. They spent around $400,000 on advertising, while they provided me with $50,000 for Amazon advertisements. I spent less, received more eyeballs on the ads, and reached impression and click rates that were 25 times greater than theirs. This example and the many others that followed were eye-opening experiences. Suddenly, I knew that Amazon was the right place, and I left—and continue to leave every meeting with brands—feeling confident in what Channel Op delivers.

Today, many of the large brands Channel Op works with see about one-third to a half of all sales revenue come from Amazon, and the advertising benefits still seem to outweigh many other marketing avenues. Because of this opportunity, many individuals and organizations wonder how far Amazon will spread its reach, questioning the lifespan and potential of such an enormous, influential corporation. To them, I say: Amazon will continue experimenting, meaning Amazon will continue expanding into diverse markets. The company has a plethora of funds to try new strategies and see what sticks. Plus, it, like many other companies such as Google, Facebook, and Apple, can identify up-and-coming ventures and acquire them. In fact, Amazon is extremely skilled at finding and procuring profitable assets. Just like how Coca-Cola and Pepsi own the majority of the largest soft drink companies, Amazon may one day claim ownership over the largest companies within various industries— technology, clothing, groceries, or whatever sector they find the most success in. The largest eCommerce site in the world, Amazon has so much of the world already underneath it that envisioning another company claiming its market share seems impossible.

With Amazon here to stay, I, as an agency founder, like the idea of Amazon taking a more agnostic approach and embracing its role as a marketplace rather than a seller itself. So far, the platform has a history of promoting its own products as cheaper alternatives to some of the best-selling items on its website. When more people begin purchasing the alternatives, the previously best-selling products are pushed down in the rankings, losing both sales and traction. While I do have process improvement notes for the platform (including more seamless movement from Vendor Central and Seller Central and more transparency concerning account fees), my most substantial wish is for Amazon to continue uplifting and empowering small businesses. In an ideal world, Amazon would simply establish an ecosystem, and sellers would populate it.

I have witnessed many brands and products attempt to populate this ecosystem over the years. Good products historically succeed, and Amazon is the optimal platform for showcasing those products, given you correctly manage all of the components that go into brand optimization. One of the most positive aspects of my career is supporting emerging companies by purchasing and trying their latest releases. These companies' leaders actively work hard to bring something original and interesting into this world; I always leave conversations with them feeling better about the trajectory of eCommerce. This level of innovation is no simple matter. On top of the hard work and monetary investment, these leaders take on a significant amount of risk and responsibility. Unlike many well-established company executives, the entrepreneurs I work with have a special kind of passion for their occupations and professional objectives. Most importantly, they approach Amazon with a sense of optimism, a vital mindset that, before the past few years, was more difficult to adopt.

The early days of Amazon felt aggressively competitive. At one time, brands struggled to usurp their competition, figuring that, if another brand outranked them, they would fade into obscurity. Now, it seems Amazon has slowly evolved to become more collaborative. Amazon optimization agencies have realized that the pie is bigger than we initially thought, so fighting over the crumbs, or brands to manage, is no longer necessary. Sharing information and industry strategies then creates a symbiotic relationship between agencies and curates a more positive environment where new brands can still find major success. This means now is the time for these smaller brands to claim their piece of the Amazon pie, taking advantage of this more constructive landscape to introduce visionary products and experiment just as Amazon does.

When I envision Channel Op's central mission, I always think about transforming Amazon into a more accessible marketplace for companies of all sizes. I want brands to launch and grow their products more easily, all while relying on a strategic partnership that guides them through any roadblocks or obstacles. A major key to this approach lies in Channel Op's internal culture and support system. By ensuring our team members feel fulfilled in their everyday work and interactions with brands, we ensure our brands feel fully supported along their own journeys. At the end of the day, our core values for the company also reflect our core values for the brands we work with—a central message that greatly inspired me to write this book in the first place.

As you read these last pages, my hope is that Channel Op's story has provided you with insight into the central pillars of Amazon brand management. I put my ideas and principles on these pages for the same reason many brands first choose to employ Channel Op's services: Amazon brand management takes decades to perfect and, most importantly, a spirit of innovation. You may have picked up this book because you wish to manage your own brand via an internal department, launch your own Amazon management company, hire a specialty brand management company, or learn more about the opportunities Amazon presents. No matter the case, know that you will need leading industry knowledge, a drive to experiment, and a dedicated team that is invested in your success. Businesses without fully developed brand management strategies will see themselves drift to the bottom of Amazon results pages. Now is the time to enact change and optimize your product page to its fullest potential, continually growing momentum on the Amazon machine.

My advice to any company involved with the Amazon marketplace is this: try something new. Purchase products that you've never tried before to see how they correlate to your own. Set ambitious objectives in the marketplace, and define a step-by-step roadmap for how to achieve them. Design and release new products on the platform to see how they perform, remembering that a lot of people who found success started their companies in their garages or basements. The opportunity is available to you, and the timing is right.

Take ownership of your Amazon today. Reap the rewards tomorrow.

ACKNOWLEDGMENTS

First off, thank you to my incredible family. To my mother, thank you for always being one phone call away. To my father, thank you for always being an example of hard work and integrity. I love you both, and I could not imagine starting a company without you in my corner.

To Nickolas, Tara, and Kaitlyn, I'm so glad that we grew up together and can still laugh for hours whenever we see each other.

To Weiran Elaine Lu, you are my favorite person, and I love the life we have built together. Trying to keep up with you has been such fun, and you are my inspiration to be better and work harder.

And to our crew, Lincoln, Brooke, Hazel, and Ezra, you kiddos are amazing, and I am so happy that I get to be alongside you as you grow up.

To Jason and JL, thanks for starting River Runners and getting me started working on Amazon.

To all of my clients, you are the reason Channel Op exists. We appreciate your trust and support, which enables us to grow our team and better serve you.

Finally, to my Channel Op team, thank you for showing up in every way. A big shout-out to Kim and Ava for your leadership. My biggest joy at work is learning from you all and seeing you all grow.

— NOTES —

1. Bastien Gauthier (General Manager of PARA'KITO), in discussion with Tyler Metcalf, July 2022.

2. Ryan Rich (Vice President of Sales and Marketing of All Good), in discussion with Tyler Metcalf, July 2022.

3. Kim Lynch (President of Channel Op), in discussion with Tyler Metcalf, August 2022.

4. Michelle Brandon (Manager of Operations of Channel Op), in discussion with Tyler Metcalf, July 2022.

5. Angela Castro (Director of Operations, Philippines Branch of Channel Op), in discussion with Tyler Metcalf, July 2022.

6. Karen Weise, "Amazon's profit soars 220 percent as pandemic drives shopping online," last modified May 12, 2021, https://www.nytimes.com/2021/04/29/technology/amazons-profits-triple.html.

7. Daphne Howland, "Amazon's e-commerce retail sales fall 3% in Q1 as consumers return to stores," April 29, 2022, https://www.retaildive.com/news/amazons-e-commerce-retail-sales-fall-3-in-q1-as-consumers-return-to-store/622920/.

8. Anna Sork, "Mapping Amazon Warehouses: How Much Square Footage Does Amazon Own?" January 7, 2022, https://www.bigrentz.com/blog/amazon-warehouses-locations.

9. Geri Mileva, "Amazon Ad Revenue Statistics That will Blow Your Mind," last modified February 23, 2022, https://influencermarketinghub.com/amazon-ad-revenue/.

10. Christine Hall and Ingrid Lunden, "Amazon aggregator Thrasio begins layoffs, names new CEO," May 2, 2022, https://techcrunch.com/2022/05/02/amazon-aggregator-thrasio-begins-layoffs-names-new-ceo/.

11. Juozas Kaziukenas, "Amazon Seller Pharmapacks Files for Bankruptcy," August 30, 2022, https://www.marketplacepulse.com/articles/top-amazon-seller-pharmapacks-files-for-bankruptcy.

ABOUT THE AUTHOR

Tyler Metcalf, CEO and founder of Channel Op, is an eCommerce branding executive who strives to provide brands with ownership over their product pages on the world's largest online selling platform, Amazon. With more than a decade of experience in Amazon page optimization, he has spearheaded unprecedented Amazon experimentation initiatives and supported industry-wide marketplace innovation.

After identifying a lack of vital communication between brand managers and their clients, Tyler founded Channel Op in 2016 to disengage from the traditional wholesale-retail model and emphasize the importance of professional partnerships. Channel Op offers a variety of services, including product page optimization, advertising, and inventory management, to foster collaboration with brands and make selling on Amazon easy. With more than $80 million in products sold and 150 total brands managed on Amazon, Channel Op now continually sees more than a 2,500% increase in client growth every four years.

Tyler received his Bachelor of Science in Economics from the University of Utah and Master of Business Administration from Babson College. He lives in Utah where he and his three children enjoy hiking, skiing, and snowboarding together.

Made in the USA
Monee, IL
18 April 2023

31644229R00052